Business Etiquette

your questions and answers

Josy Roberts

TROTMAN

About the Author

Josy Roberts has worked in administrative, marketing and management roles over the last 15 years for a variety of organisations, including family-owned small businesses, charities and major corporations. As well as the scars of experience she holds an honours degree in Sociology, a marketing certificate and Diploma in Management.

She believes strongly that the success of organisations and individuals – whatever they do – is based on communications skills and a professional approach, and with that the working day can and should be enjoyable.

This first edition published in 1998 in Great Britain by Trotman and Company Limited, 12 Hill Rise, Richmond, Surrey TW10 6UA
© Trotman and Company Limited 1998

British Library Cataloguing in Publication Data
A catalogue record for this book is available from the British Library
ISBN 0 85660 329 5

All rights reserved. No part of this publication may be reproduced, stored in a retrieval system or transmitted in any form or by any means, electronic and mechanical, photocopying, recording or otherwise without prior permission of Trotman and Company Limited.

Printed and bound in Great Britain by Redwood Books

Contents

1.	**What is business etiquette?**	**1**
	Why do you need to know about business etiquette?	2
2.	**How do I make a good impression?**	**4**
	How should I dress for business?	5
	What are some rules of good business behaviour?	7
	How do I deal with criticism?	9
3.	**How should I use different types of communication?**	**11**
	How should I handle phone calls?	12
	How should I deal with messages and voicemail?	13
	What about mobile phones?	14
	How should I use email?	15
	How should I write business letters?	16
	How do I use facsimile?	18
	When would I send a memo	19
	What are business cards and compliment slips used for?	19
	When would I need a face-to-face meeting?	20
4.	**What do I need to know about behaviour at work?**	**21**
	How do I arrange holidays or time off?	22
	How do I take lunch and other breaks?	23
	How do I deal with personal property and shared space?	23
	How do I ask for a salary rise or other benefits?	27
	What is antisocial behaviour?	28
5.	**How do I deal with business contacts and customers?**	**31**
	How do I arrange a meeting?	31
	How do I run a meeting?	33
	How do I make introductions?	35
	What about going to conferences and exhibitions?	36

How should I behave at a business lunch or dinner?	37
What about business gifts?	39
What business etiquette rules do I need to consider with international contacts?	40
6. Where can I find out more?	**42**
Is there any special training?	42
Who could I contact?	42
What publications should I look at?	43

Business Etiquette *your questions and answers*

1. What is business etiquette?

Etiquette means 'conventional rules of polite behaviour'. Wherever you work there will be other people inside and outside your organisation who you deal with and it is crucial to communicate with them well. A key part of this is to show your respect in the appropriate way, and conform to the largely unwritten guidelines on behaviour. The more you understand the rules, the more comfortable you will be in any business situation.

Business etiquette covers a very wide range of things:

- How you behave as an individual
- How you make use of the communication tools available
- How you act in the team and company that you work in
- How you deal with external business contacts.

There are some general commandments of good manners that we all understand. For instance, there are very few workplaces where swearing or poor personal hygiene are approved of. Using the office telephone to set up a private dating agency or taking your pet tarantula into work for exercise is likely to be frowned upon. Stretching out on the sofa in reception and having a nap will raise a few eyebrows.

Every company has slightly different conventions about appropriate conduct. Remember that when you start a job it's a bit like joining a new club. Some of the rules might be written down but everyone else knows the other members and how to act with them. You have to learn it all if you are going to enjoy being there.

Some companies have very formal practices and others are more casual. A large government department is likely to have more rules written down than a small design company. A checklist of things you should find out about would include:

- Is there a company style for memos and letters?
- Is there a company dress code?
- What happens about coffee and lunch breaks?
- How are managers addressed – by title or first name?
- How do I request holidays or time off?

When you attend an interview, or start a new job, the best advice is to conduct yourself with more formal or 'proper' behaviour. You can always relax into more casual dress or speech if you can see that this is normal.

Why do you need to know about business etiquette?

How you look, act, speak and write gives people around you an impression. Think about sitting on a train and looking at the other people in the carriage. You have immediately written a story in your head about what they are like, and whether you would get on with them. The loud mouth sounding off to his friends about his latest conquest, or the individual holding a very personal conversation on her mobile phone might be interesting for a moment – but not something you would like to see or listen to every day.

Imagine going to a business meeting where everyone behaved as if they were on a train. In business that first impression is significantly more important. Unlike the train, we can't move to the next carriage or get off at the next stop. The people you work with will see and speak to you frequently. Customers will expect helpfulness and civility when you meet them. Bosses will expect you to be courteous.

In the last 15 years workplaces have become much more informal – most people are called by their first names, for instance, and dress codes are much less rigid in many industries. There has been a removal of hierarchy and a move to flatter organisations with fewer supervisors and managers. This doesn't mean that less respectful behaviour towards others is sanctioned, it's just that the rules aren't so obvious.

What matters most is that your behaviour, dress, speech and other communications with your colleagues and customers are appropriate for your job and the company you work for. The office of a small, family-run taxi firm might be a lot more relaxed than a London-based limousine company, but the principles remain the same.

Business people often talk about 'networking', which is about building up ongoing relationships with contacts who may be useful in the future. Understanding good business etiquette is essential in setting up your own network and keeping it going.

Knowing how to behave, with politeness and courtesy, is a very important part of business life. Using business etiquette to create the right impression will determine not only how you enjoy each working day, but also your chances of promotion and success in your career.

Business Etiquette your questions and answers

2. How do I make a good impression?

The first place you need to make a good impression is at the job interview. What are the things to consider?

- ❏ Turning up on time
- ❏ How you are dressed
- ❏ Body language – how you shake hands, stand or sit
- ❏ How you talk to the person interviewing you
    - Do you make eye contact and smile?
    - Do you speak clearly without pausing or using slang?
    - Are you prepared for the questions?
    - Do you have prepared questions of your own?

The impression you give will be a combination of a number of things – how you look, how you manage your body, how you listen, how you speak and ask questions, how you respond to challenges and how you deal with negative feedback.

Interviews are a very good model for thinking about how you act at any business meeting. All of the same rules apply about how the person you are meeting sees you and the company you are representing.

So making a good impression is about:

- ❏ Dressing and acting appropriately
- ❏ Being prepared
- ❏ Communicating well

Business Etiquette *your questions and answers*

How should I dress for business?

Grooming

A clean and tidy appearance is crucial if you want to be taken seriously at work. If you visited a bank and all the cashiers looked as if they had just finished a game of football or been sleeping rough you might not feel too confident about your money in their hands.

Good grooming means looking after every aspect of your appearance – hair, nails, and personal hygiene – as well as your choice of clothes and accessories.

Hair should always be clean and tidy. Regular haircuts are important for men as well as women. Loose hair flopping over your eyes might be fashionable, but it blocks eye contact. People who are continually playing with their hair, or tossing their heads like horses to get it out of the way, seem nervous and distracted. Strange colours and hair accessories might be appropriate if you work in a nightclub, but they don't fit in at most offices.

Men should always be well shaven, or with neatly trimmed moustaches and beards. (In cartoons dark stubble is used to show who the bad-guys are.)

Hands, face and teeth should always be clean. If you read a newspaper on the way to work check that black smudges haven't transferred from your hands to your face.

Fingernails must always be clean and well shaped. Nail polish for women is fine providing it is in a pale colour, and isn't chipped or cracked. Nail polish on men might be open to misinterpretation.

The human sense of smell has a very powerful impact on our emotions. Most people have a very strong reaction to body odour, the aroma of musty clothes or bad breath. Use a deodorant if you work in close quarters with others. Never use perfume or aftershave to cover smells, and don't overuse any fragrance product. The famous series of ads with men 'acting on impulse' started with the assumption that they hadn't gagged to death inhaling. Smoking causes unpleasant breath so if you are an addict, brush your teeth before meetings or make use of breath-freshening mints.

Your clothes should always be clean and pressed. Stains, dandruff, hairs, cat fur, food particles, missing buttons, splitting seams, frayed cuffs, corrugated wrinkles, scuffed shoes or fallen hems are noticed, particularly if you consistently look messy.

Choosing your wardrobe for work

You may be required to wear a uniform for work, or a certain colour shirt with trousers or skirt, for instance if you work for an airline, a building society or chain store, or one of the emergency services. This makes your choice of clothes easier in the morning, but the same rules of cleanliness apply – especially as you are immediately identified with a particular company or organisation. You may also be required to wear a certain type of clothing to do your job or for safety reasons – for instance, if you work in a kitchen, hospital, laboratory or factory protective clothing is a requirement under health and safety regulations.

In other fields there is a type of outfit or uniform that is acceptable in the office world. Standard business dress for men is a suit and tie, with a plain colour collared shirt and dark shoes. In the city or professional firms, such as law and banking, dark suits or pinstripes are expected. In media or advertising companies less formal coloured suits or jackets and trousers are often worn.

For women the choices are broader – a suit or a skirt and jacket with a blouse is always acceptable. Tailored dresses are frequently worn; many companies accept trousers. Avoid disco gear – tight clothing with very short skirts and low necklines, or exposed mid-drifts, jangley jewellery or bondage style footwear are inappropriate in the workplace.

Dress codes at work vary depending on the company and industry you work in, and the type of job you have. If you are meeting customers frequently then you are more likely to need formal office clothing. Don't let the polished look down with trainers and a carrier bag instead of a briefcase.

Business executives, television presenters and professional advisers often invest in style consultants, who help define and choose the most appropriate and attractive colours and shapes in clothing for the individual.

Many companies publish guidelines in their staff handbooks which outline business dress and list the no-nos – for instance jeans, cropped tee-shirts, shorts or leggings are normally banned. Some organisations do have official 'dressing down' or 'mufti' days where casual clothes are allowed. If you are in doubt ask your manager, and look at what your colleagues are wearing. Use your own judgement too – examine yourself in a mirror – do you look like your job?

What are some rules of good business behaviour?

Punctuality
Be on time. If you are attending a meeting, or have fixed hours of work, always arrive at least five minutes early – so you are ready to start at the right time. Keeping people waiting creates resentment which isn't forgotten, however good your excuse or craven your apology.

Handshakes and greetings
When you are meeting people for the first time greet them professionally. Introduce yourself, extend your right hand in a positive motion, and as you shake hands say 'pleased to meet you' or 'how do you do', and smile.

Remember names
Remember the names of the people you meet, and call them by name when you address them. A good trick is to make sure you repeat their name slowly, at least in your head, when you are introduced. Don't get

it wrong – if you think you have forgotten, don't use the name until you have had time to double-check with a colleague.

Body language

When talking or listening, smile, and make eye contact with the speaker. (This doesn't mean pretend you are doing a screen test for a film about a psychopath – be genuine.) If you have papers with you or are taking notes make sure you look up frequently and nod or smile to show you are concentrating on the people in the room.

Use your posture to show your interest and alertness. Sit or stand upright – not slouched in your chair or resting your head on your hand. Both men and women should keep their legs together regardless of clothing. Don't cross your arms – this is a defensive position.

Listening skills

Listening isn't just about being quiet while other people speak – make sure you understand what is being said. Don't interrupt a speaker, but if a pause occurs phrase a question politely, or repeat your understanding of what was said and ask if it is correct. For example, 'Excuse me Miss Print, do you mean that you are looking for a candidate who can use desktop publishing packages?'

Thanks and recognition

Always thank a person if they have given you anything, whether it's information or coffee, or helped you in anyway – from proofreading a report to opening a door for you. Courtesy costs nothing, and the lack of it is always noticed.

Sensitivity to others

There are hundreds of funny stories about inappropriate behaviour – the person who fell asleep during an interview, the man who took out his hearing aid and cleaned it during a meeting, or the woman who had the back of her skirt caught in her tights. Accidents happen and are usually just embarrassing, but deliberate behaviour that can cause offence to others is unacceptable.

Business Etiquette *your questions and answers*

Here are some things that deserve very big black marks in any business situation:

- ✖ Getting up and leaving a room without explanation or apology.
- ✖ Staring out of the window, yawning or falling asleep.
- ✖ Shouting, getting angry or annoyed.
- ✖ Openly criticising anyone, whether it's your previous employer, the receptionist or a colleague.
- ✖ Taking telephone calls on a mobile phone during a meeting.
- ✖ Swearing or making suggestive or personal remarks. ('That's an immense spot on your nose, isn't it?')
- ✖ Using over-familiar names – luv, guv, dear, mate, sweetie, darling, will all offend someone.
- ✖ Interrupting anyone while they are speaking.
- ✖ Scratching your body or fiddling with your hair, skin or clothing – or any emission of bodily gases.
- ✖ Adjusting your personal appearance – buttoning a shirt, cleaning your nails, picking your teeth, or combing your hair. Do all of that in the toilets in private.

How do I deal with criticism?

In everyone's working life there are times when criticisms are made. They can be difficult to hear however carefully worded. The key thing to remember is to separate your emotional reaction from what is actually being said. Criticism is not usually directed at your character but at some aspect of your work that could be improved (and unless you're employed in a family business, it's unlikely to be your mother speaking).

However surprised or upset you might be, behave with dignity. Listen carefully and don't react immediately and angrily – control your temper. Colleagues and managers will give a person who flies off the handle a very wide berth.

Think about what was said. Is it justified? If necessary ask for time to consider the comments made. Show that you take it seriously by asking for suggestions or help in improving. By exhibiting a willingness to change and listen to advice you will increase you chances of extra training and promotion.

Let's take an example: your manager takes you to one side and says, 'I think the report you wrote for me was a bit slapdash, and missed some important points.'

Do you hit the roof and say, 'Well I thought it was fine… and you didn't give me enough time… and my computer doesn't work… and I didn't have a proper briefing… and no one would help me… and I've had too much other work to do… and the office is too noisy for me to concentrate… and I'm not paid enough… DON'T PICK ON ME!'

Or do you take a deep breath and say, 'I did write it in a hurry, and I might have been a bit confused about what you wanted. Can you show me where you think I went wrong, and perhaps someone could help me with it?'

If you feel you are receiving continued and unjustified fault-finding – or any type of harassment – from a manager or colleague, then you should handle it professionally, without becoming too emotional. A first step is to ask to speak to the individual privately, explain that you feel their comments are not merited, and try to reach an understanding. It is best to try to deal with the person directly first rather than escalate the problem to their manager.

If you need to take the matter further, go to your immediate supervisor or manager in private. In larger companies there is usually a personnel department to talk to or an established complaints procedure.

What you should avoid at all costs is entering into a public argument, or spending a lot of time moaning to other workmates.

3. How should I use different types of communication?

When you work in an office there are many different ways of communicating with colleagues and external contacts, both to request and receive information. There is the telephone, voicemail and message centres, letters, faxes, emails, or face-to-face contact.

There are two golden rules:
1. Choose the most appropriate means for the messages you have to relay, and be as clear and brief as possible.
2. Don't use the business communication tools provided by your employer for your personal life.

Checklist of communication methods

	Telephone	Email	Letter or report	Fax	Memo	Meeting
Is it urgent?	✓	✓		✓		
Is a discussion needed?	✓					✓
Is it official – like a quote or report?			✓		✓	
Is it internal?	✓	✓			✓	✓
Is it going to many people?		✓			✓	
Is it confidential?			✓		✓	

Business Etiquette *your questions and answers*

For instance:

- If you are confirming the date, time and location of an internal meeting then the most effective means of sending the information is via email or a memo.
- If you are sending someone confidential financial information or statistics, then use a letter or memo in a sealed envelope marked 'Private'.
- If you need to confirm the address or date of a meeting – telephone!

How should I handle phone calls?

We all know how to use the telephone – pick up a handset, dial and speak. But that is not enough to appear professional. Here are some quick tips.

- When you answer the phone start with a greeting, so the caller gets used to your voice, state your company or department, and your name clearly, and then ask them to speak.

  'Good morning, TV Productions Limited, Beverly Hills speaking, how can I help you?'

- Sit up straight and smile while you are talking – it sounds silly but makes a great difference to the tone of your voice.
- Don't eat a sandwich, chew gum, smoke or drink a coffee while speaking.
- If you have limited time to talk, explain to the caller that you must leave shortly and arrange a time to call them back, or ask a colleague to take a message.
- Speak clearly and briefly – don't ramble on.
- Never interrupt the other person while they are talking.
- Always have a notepad and pen near the phone so you can jot down important points during the conversation. Note the caller's name immediately so you can address them personally as you speak.

Business Etiquette *your questions and answers*

How should I deal with messages and voicemail?

Taking a message for colleagues
If you answer the phone for someone else, state the company or department name, and the person whose phone you are answering.

> 'Good morning Military Accessories Ltd, Jenny Rall's desk – can I help you?'

If you can handle the query then deal with it yourself. If not, write down who called, the time, their phone number and a brief summary of their question. Make sure you leave the message in an obvious place on the desk so it will be easily seen, such as on a notepad next to the telephone. Post-it notes stuck to the telephone or computer screen may seem like a good idea, but they make it difficult to use the equipment and get lost easily.

Storing a greeting on voicemail
If you have voicemail or answerphones at work there are two ways of storing messages, depending on the availability of colleagues to deal with your calls:

- ❏ Set a standard message explaining that you are not currently available and ask callers to leave a message or contact another person.

  > 'Hello this is Walt Senall in office services. Please leave a message, and I will get back to you as soon as I can, or dial extension 3456 for urgent attention.'

- ❏ Change your message daily, explaining whether you are in the office and temporarily unavailable, or away.

  > 'Hello this is Denise Nocke on Tuesday the 17th of March. I will be out of the office until Friday. Please leave a message and I will return your call when I get back.'

  If you do store a message with a date in it you must update it regularly.

Business Etiquette *your questions and answers*

- It is good practice to return a call within the working day – so set time aside to deal with phone calls if you get a lot of them.

Leaving a message

As companies make more and more use of technology, and have fewer secretaries and telephone staff, it is very likely you will speak to a machine when making phone calls. So be prepared before you dial to listen to automated operators, and to leave an effective message:

- Make a note of the key points before you dial, so you can leave a message without pausing to think.
- Speak clearly and brightly – sit up straight!
- Say your name in full, and the company you are calling from.
- Say your telephone number slowly enough so the listener can write it down first time and doesn't need to listen to the message again.
- Say why you are calling, but be brief and don't ramble – a long meaningless message that can't be fast-forwarded is frustrating for the recipient.

If it helps you to be concise and not forget the key points (like your name!), write out your message first so you can read it if you need to.

What about mobile phones?

Mobile telephones are extremely useful communication devices for business people who travel, or are away from their office frequently. They can also be a source of intense irritation for others – even blinding rage – if used inappropriately.

If you have a mobile phone:

- Make sure it has a suitable message service.
- Switch it off when you are unable to speak – for instance in meetings or when driving.
- Unless it's absolutely necessary, switch it off in restaurants and other social venues. Some restaurants ban mobile telephones now.

Business Etiquette *your questions and answers*

- Keep conversations short and to the point.
- Try to find somewhere private and quiet before making a call.
- Don't make a call if the reception is bad or your batteries are low – it creates frustration for the person on the other end of the line.

If you are calling a mobile phone telephone number:

- Find out where the receiver is and if they are able to talk.
- Be prepared to leave a message.
- Recognise that the person you are speaking to may be in a public place, so might not want to have a long detailed or contentious conversation.

How should I use email?

Emails are a very effective way of sending information. They are fast, efficient and much cheaper than sending material by post or fax. However, because email is so easy to use, it is tempting to be a bit careless or casual when tapping a note to someone. Remember – you have no idea what kind of mood they will be in, or how many other emails they have to deal with, so:

- Always put an appropriate title in the subject field, so the reader knows what it is about before opening.
- Email is very unforgiving – you must get the address exactly right.
- Use good English and correct spelling.
- Be polite and concise.
- Avoid sending large attachments – many companies put a limit on the size of messages.
- If you send attachments make sure the person you are sending it to has a version of software that can read it.

And avoid the following:

✘ Never send a message that is defamatory or could be offensive. There are already many cases of legal action being taken because

Business Etiquette *your questions and answers*

of improper messages – like rude jokes that have been circulated and have been considered sexual harassment.

- ✘ Don't expect an immediate response – some people check their email more frequently than others do.
- ✘ Don't send a message marked 'urgent' if it isn't.
- ✘ Don't copy to everyone indiscriminately. It is very easy to send an email to hundreds of people – but do they need to receive it?
- ✘ Don't use email to avoid speaking to someone.
- ✘ Don't add 'emoticons' – smiley faces or graphics to show a mood. That's fun in primary school.

Your should create your own system to deal with your email efficiently. For example, check your mailbox at set times during the day, and always allow enough time to deal with urgent messages.

Delete messages or store them in a subject folder once you have dealt with them, so your inbox remains clear.

How should I write business letters?

A business letter is a formal document, written on the company's headed paper. It is likely to be saved and filed by the sender and the receiver as a record of an event or transaction, so it must be correct. It also shows the professionalism of both the writer and the writer's company to clients and other external contacts, so sloppy language and spelling errors should be avoided.

There are many reasons to write a business letter – to seek information or opinion, to place or confirm an order, to sell a company's products, to offer information in response to an enquiry, to provide a quotation, to make a complaint or to respond to a complaint.

Here are some examples:

❑ An individual has telephoned your company and asked for details of your products or services.

- A customer has written a letter complaining about a product or service provided by your company.
- You are responding to a job advertisement in a newspaper.
- You have been to a meeting and the client asked for more information on a subject, which you are sending to them.

To write a good business letter you must:

- Use appropriate layout – with all the formal elements. These include a date, name and address, salutation ('Dear —'), body of the letter, complimentary close ('Yours sincerely/faithfully), your name and your job title.
- Make sure you get the right name, address and title of the person you are writing to. If in doubt use 'Mr' for men and 'Ms' for women with their last name. First try to find out their correct title, especially if you are writing to a non-English speaking country, or if you are not sure of the person's gender.
- Put a heading on your letter, so the reader can immediately see what it is about.
- Keep it short – one page or at most two is enough. If you have a lot of information to give someone, enclose it as a report or brochure.
- Use clear English – the correct grammar, and the right vocabulary for your reader. Avoid jargon that might not be understood and long-winded phrases that don't say anything.
- Make the style and tone of your writing appropriate for the messages and the reader.
- Ensure the content of your letter is correct and relevant.
- Don't forget to sign the letter before posting, as this personalises it and gives it authority.

Many organisations have an established house-style for letter layout and vocabulary. They may also publish guidelines on who should write and sign letters on behalf of the company. If you are not sure, check with your manager or personnel department before sending out a letter.

Business Etiquette your questions and answers

How do I use facsimile?

Fax is short for 'facsimile', which means 'exact copy'. Fax is a means of sending copies of documents instantly down a telephone line, rather than a specific type of communication. If you are sending a letter or, for instance a map, which is urgent, then fax is more convenient for the recipient because they will get it immediately.

Fax machines tend to be shared in offices – so confidential information should not be sent unless you have agreed with someone to collect it immediately.

You should always prepare a covering sheet with the name, telephone number of the person it is addressed to, and your own details. Some companies have pre-printed cover sheets, or word-processor templates to use. Here is an example of a 'cover sheet'.

FACSIMILE

To:	Fran Ticke	Tel:	01731 567910
	Eco Publishing Ltd	Fax:	01731 567900
From:	Percy Vere	Tel:	01992 468024
	Kallory Catering	Fax:	01992 468022

Date: 4th July 1998   Number of pages: 6

Message:

Fran,
Here is a selection of our set meals for you to choose the menu for your office party next Friday. Several vegetarian options are included…

If you are sending a number of pages with the fax, it is a good idea to say how many pages are included on the cover sheet, and number each page, so the recipient can tell if there is anything missing.

Business Etiquette *your questions and answers*

When would I send a memo?

Memos should only be sent within a company – they are internal documents printed on plain paper, not letter heading. Some appropriate uses of memos might be:

- A personnel department sends a memo to all staff outlining a new training policy.
- A manager pins a memo on the noticeboard announcing the appointment of a new member of staff.
- A colleague sends you a memo responding to a request for information.

Email is increasingly used in place of memos, especially in larger companies where staff all have email, and a memo would be time consuming to photocopy and distribute.

What are business cards and compliment slips used for?

Business cards generally contain a person's name, job title, company address, telephone number, fax and email address. They are exchanged when people from different companies introduce themselves – at meetings or conferences, or networking at business events.

When you meet with a lot of new people business cards are very useful to help remember names. For example, at a meeting you could put the cards out next to you in the order that people are sitting so you can glance at them easily and get the names right.

A very useful thing to do is jot down on the back of the card the date you met, and some points about the meeting or person. Many people store business cards in special folders, or keep them in a card index box with all their contact names and addresses.

Compliment slips are used when you are sending information or material to a business contact and a formal letter isn't necessary. Some people just sign their name, or have it printed on the slip. It is more personal to write a brief message and useful to include the date.

When would I need a face-to-face meeting?

If you need to share a lot of information with others in your company, or talk to a client about tailoring your service or product to their specific needs, it may be more effective to meet face to face. Unlike written communications, meetings allow for questioning, discussion, negotiation, and immediate feedback. To be productive rather than a rambling waste of time, they do need to be carefully structured and managed. A large meeting should have an agenda to stick to, and someone 'chairing' or leading the conversation. A one-to-one meeting is less likely to go off the rails, but should still have a clear focus, and preparation is needed.

Arranging and running business meetings with people outside your company are covered on pages 31–34. But there are many reasons why you will need formal meetings within your own company. Here are a few examples:

- Your department has regular fortnightly or monthly meetings to ensure everyone is up to date with work in progress.
- You have regular meetings with other departments to share information on specific projects.
- Your director organises a meeting to make a special announcement to all staff.
- You have an annual appraisal with your manager or supervisor.

4. What do I need to know about behaviour at work?

Wherever you work, other people will surround you – colleagues you share space or facilities with, who you see every day. Good relationships with the people in your workplace will help you do your job better, and can be a great source of fun. On the flip side, it's like families or a class at school – you can't choose the people around you, and conflicts do cause problems and create unhappiness. Think how often you have heard your friends or relatives complain about someone they work with.

There are some very simple things to keep in mind:

- Companies very often have written policies on a range of things, from taking holidays to keeping your desk tidy – find out what they are and follow them.
- Not everyone you work with will be your best friend, but you'll have to adjust to them, be with them for several hours a day, and be able to ask for help if you need it.
- Be courteous. Say 'good morning' even if it isn't. Ask to borrow the stapler rather than just taking it.
- Don't impede someone else's ability to do their job. Creating unnecessary noise, monopolising shared equipment like the fax machine, or using all the paper in the photocopier without refilling it, will very soon gain you a reputation as a pain in the neck.

- Be considerate. If you are away from your desk, who will have to answer the phone? If you want to take holiday, who will cover your work? Make sure that they agree to helping you.

How do I arrange holidays or time off?

When you start a new job you will be told how many days holiday you can take in a calendar year. Some employers set guidelines about how many days can be taken at one time, how approval is requested or how much notice you need to give, so check with your manager.

If you are arranging a holiday you must clear it with your employer, as far in advance as possible, before buying the plane tickets, or booking the cruise. It is not practical for 50% of staff to be away at the same time – particularly if it is during a busy period. Some workplaces use wall charts or electronic diaries so you can find out if others already have the time booked.

Colleagues with children are usually restricted to school breaks for their holidays. If you have more flexibility it is considerate (and often cheaper) to avoid the peak periods.

If you are requesting one or two days off at short notice, check this doesn't conflict with your work commitments before asking for the leave.

Sometimes emergencies take place in your home or family and you need time off at very short notice. Most employers are understanding about these events, providing it is a true emergency, and you contact your manager as soon as possible so your work can be covered. They are less sympathetic with people who are constantly taking sick leave for minor aches and pains – it means you're not dependable and puts strain on other members of staff.

Companies usually have formal sickness reporting procedures, which define who you should contact, and when a doctor's note is needed.

Business Etiquette *your questions and answers*

How do I take lunch and other breaks?

Depending on the type of business you work in, arrangements for taking lunch or coffee breaks will be fixed or flexible. For instance if the cashiers on the till in the supermarket just got up and went for lunch without getting cover, customers wouldn't be too happy.

- Find out how breaks are organised in your company.
- Never take longer than the 45 minutes or hour allocated for lunch, unless you have had approval.
- Tell your colleagues or manager that you are taking a break – don't just disappear.
- Make sure your telephone is switched to voicemail, or someone has agreed to answer it for you.

How do I deal with personal property and shared space?

It is very tempting to personalise your working area – put up a picture of your favourite football player or sexy movie star, have a few toys sitting on your desk, add a small rug beneath your chair… perhaps some curtains and soft music and lighting…

Wrong. Your working space is not a private den or play centre with hundreds of distractions – it's somewhere to do work. You wouldn't feel very comfortable if a bus driver had a Nintendo Game Boy in the cab, and Lara Croft posters on the windscreen.

Many offices are open plan, so you share space, light and noise with all the people around you. Use your common sense about what is likely to be irritating or unpleasant for others.

Tidiness

Keep your work area tidy – put rubbish in the bin, files, books and materials on shelves or in cupboards. Don't block walkways and clear up your work surface at the end of each day. If you've had to use extra space for a task and your work has spilled over into common areas or on to someone else's desk, make sure it's cleared away as soon as you've finished the job.

Light

Don't block natural light by putting material up on windows or glass partitions. Don't turn off overhead lights without checking with others.

Telephone and office conversations

Speak clearly when on the telephone or consulting with your workmates, but watch the volume. Don't hold loud conversations about personal details, screech, laugh hysterically, shout or swear.

Food and drink

Depending on the policy of the company you work for, coffee, soft drinks and sandwiches may be consumed at your workstation. But never leave half-finished refreshments or dirty cups and plates around to rot, and avoid bringing in food with strong smells.

If you have a kitchen area for making coffee and tea, take some responsibility for its cleanliness. Put milk back in the fridge and wash up your own mugs. Don't leave your yoghurt/tuna sandwich/cheese selection/mixed salad in the fridge for six months.

Health and safety

While it is polite to behave with sensitivity to colleagues, health and safety regulations exist which protect your rights as an employee. Employers have a legal requirement to provide a safe workplace. They must ensure that any machinery is safe to use, that proper training is provided, that access to and from work areas is clear and that the working environment is safe generally.

Employees are required to take reasonable care and cooperate with health and safety guidelines.

- ❑ You must keep work areas tidy, and ensure that no materials or furniture block passageways and emergency exits.

Business Etiquette *your questions and answers*

- You should make sure you know the emergency exit procedures and fire drills should happen at least once a year.
- Electrical equipment must be inspected, and cables need to be covered. Many employers forbid that repairs or alterations are carried out by anyone other than a qualified technician, and ban employees bringing in their own equipment like desk lights, fans or audio equipment.
- You must report any damage or spillage on floor coverings immediately.
- You must ensure that no filing or storage furniture is overloaded or doors and drawers are left open.
- You should behave sensibly – don't wear garments that will catch on furniture or equipment; be alert, don't run around corners or burst through doors like superman; and use the equipment you have been provided with for what it is designed for – standing on a revolving chair to reach a high shelf might be expedient but it's not very clever.
- In some jobs protective equipment or clothing will be provided, like eye protectors, rubber gloves, overalls. Make sure you use them.

Visitors to your workplace

If you have a business contact visiting your place of work in order to find out more about your organisation, make sure your colleagues and managers know about it in advance. Arrange the visit for a convenient time – not when there is a fire drill, a big work deadline or office charity fancy dress competition going on. Make sure that colleagues know they should put away confidential information, and make preparations to give a good impression.

Introduce visitors to the relevant people they should meet – the ones they might be working with or speak to on the phone. They probably won't need to shake hands with the security guard or cleaning staff. Keep the tour short – if detailed discussions are necessary arrange a meeting room rather than disrupting your colleagues for a long time.

Business Etiquette *your questions and answers*

Non-work visitors

Because you spend so much of your life working it is very tempting to involve elements of your personal life in the workplace. Approach this with caution. First check with your manager whether there is a policy about visitors to you offices – there may be health and safety or business reasons why visitors are not allowed.

It is nice to introduce your partner, mother or best friend to your close work colleagues so they know more about you. An extended visit with tea and cakes during the working day is not on. Arrange for greetings to be made at the beginning of a lunch break or at the end of the day.

Unless you are employed in a crèche or veterinary clinic bringing children or animals into work with you to care for them is not generally acceptable. In a very unusual emergency you could ask your supervisor, but it is a very rare organisation which would give permission as it inevitably disrupts other staff.

The politically correct personal computer (or the pc PC)

Computers are fun – machines can now be customised with all sorts of noises, and pictures – even play CDs. But the person next to you might not think that the sound of someone blowing a raspberry when you make a mistake is that funny after the 456th time.

Computers are business tools to help people do their jobs. Spending working time playing games or surfing the Internet for pictures of Mel Gibson naked is not an appropriate use of resources and creates a very poor impression of your commitment to your work.

How do I ask for a salary rise or other benefits?

Your relationship to your employer is a contract. You agree to do a certain amount of work everyday to benefit the company, and they agree to pay you. When you join an organisation you will probably be told how salaries are set and reviewed. Some organisations have annual pay rises for all staff; some have established salary bands depending on job grades; and some link pay increased to performance reviews or promotions.

If you are unsure, ask your manager or personnel department in confidence. It is not a good idea, and is unlikely to get the result you want, to stand up in the middle of a crowded room and yell 'I want more money' (even with a semi-automatic weapon in your hand).

The best time to ask for a salary review or extra training and development is during an appraisal with your manager. If the organisation doesn't have a calendar for appraisals then ask for a meeting with your manager.

Explain clearly and unemotionally why you think a review is needed, and why you are worth more to the company. For example, 'Over the last six months I have taken on extra work and I am now responsible for all the end of month accounts without assistance. I would like you to consider increasing my salary to reflect this.'

'Please give me a pay rise because I fancy a new sportscar' doesn't do it for most managers.

What is antisocial behaviour?

Your common sense will tell you that illegal activities, like drug taking, murder or vandalism clearly have no place in business, unless you work for the criminal fraternity.

There are a few real first division taboos which are universally unacceptable in the workplace: drunkenness, smoking outside of a designated area, and sexual harassment.

Alcohol

Being drunk during working hours and unable to do your job for most employers is considered an instantly sackable offence. Some companies now prohibit any drinking at lunchtime. Drinking is a social activity, and should be kept to your social life out of work hours. A glass of wine at a business lunch is acceptable, a bottle of vodka with a colleague to speed up a Monday afternoon is not.

Smoking

The health risks associated with smoking and passive smoking are extremely well publicised, and a nicotine addict is more of a social pariah now than a plague victim. If one person in an office or meeting is a non-smoker then everyone else should refrain from lighting up. Some organisations ban smoking altogether, while others have set up designated smoking areas.

If you need to smoke during the day, then take breaks with consideration of others in mind. Trooping off *en masse* to the smoking room with your friends to have a chat causes frustration for those left behind who have to answer the phone, and implies you don't take your job very seriously.

Sexual harassment

It is not permissible to touch, grab, pinch or tickle any colleague – of the opposite sex or otherwise. Rude suggestive comments and obvious eyeing up are unacceptable too. For some people the line between flirtation or joking and offensive behaviour is hard to recognise, but you shouldn't be forced to tolerate behaviour from others that genuinely makes you uncomfortable.

Sometimes it's easy to get across the message that you think someone's behaviour is out of line – by refusing to smile, saying 'please don't do that' or avoiding them.

Before you escalate the problem into a formal complaint and legal action, it is worth trying to explain that you find the specific attention unacceptable, and ask him or her to stop. If this doesn't work you must make a formal complaint and report the situation to a personnel manager.

Other taboos

Second division bad behaviour includes poor punctuality, gossip and rumour mongering, and letting private life clashes dominate over work responsibilities – 'I've got to leave early to get my hair done… service the car… get ready for a party…' All of these examples show that you are not serious about your job, or honouring the employment contract.

Discretion is important for your relationships with colleagues, and if you cannot be trusted on a personal level, you will find you are not trusted professionally either. So if you are told something in confidence, honour the promise you have made and keep it to yourself. Outside the office do not criticise the company or your colleagues to other organisations. Don't share private or sensitive information with people who could use it against you or the company.

Political correctness

Being 'pc' or politically correct is the focus of a lot of comedians' jokes, about 'right-on' local councils or lobbying groups. It's a very buzzy concept which sits somewhere between being sensitive to your environment and being fashionable – or rather combining the two!

There are sound aims behind political correctness. A politically correct person does not speak or act in a way that a person of another race, religion or gender would find offensive. It is not politically correct to discriminate against a person based on race, religion, physical or mental handicap or sexual preferences.

When you are at work there will be many people around you who feel strongly or uncomfortable about certain issues. Show your respect by avoiding subjects or jokes likely to cause offence.

While you don't necessarily have to embrace or become fanatical about all the current causes – like green issues such as water pollution, reducing road traffic, road development protests, animal testing, vegetarianism or energy conservation – be aware that all of the movements are motivated by the desire to improve society and the world, so deserve some respect.

Business Etiquette *your questions and answers*

5. How do I deal with business contacts and customers?

Good relationships with colleagues are very important, but even more crucial for your career development and the company's success is how you act with external contacts.

The most frequent situation you will find yourself in is business meetings. As a start, learn how to arrange a meeting professionally – it will give a good impression before contacts have even met you.

Handling formal introductions correctly is another important social skill, and sets the tone for any subsequent conversation.

There are other events where business contacts are made, such as conferences and exhibitions, and lunches and dinners. Behaviour at such events will be a combination of good professional conduct, social skills and common sense.

How do I arrange a meeting?

Business meetings are very useful face-to-face exchanges with contacts outside the company, but if they are not professionally handled they can be a waste of time and give a damaging impression. If it's your job to arrange a meeting, make sure you follow these simple rules.

1. Decide on the purpose of the meeting – it should have a clear focus or specific points to address.
2. Write a list of who should be present – think who will make a contribution. Don't invite people who have no reason to be there.
3. Contact each person by telephone to find a convenient time for everyone. Allow enough time for travel if individuals are coming from long distances. A good tip is to start with three to four suggested dates and confirm availability. Mornings are generally a better time for meetings – unless that's inappropriate for the business, for instance an office catering company might only be able to meet after lunch because the morning is a busy work time for them.
4. Ask participants if they need any special equipment and check the systems they use. Ask them if they have any suggestions for the agenda.
5. Book a meeting room – ensuring it is large enough for the group – and arrange the appropriate equipment, and refreshments.
6. Write an agenda and circulate it to everyone who will be attending. An agenda is a list of topics that the meeting will cover, and normally includes suggested times for each item. It is important to structure the order logically, and start with routine items. A simple agenda might be:

```
AGENDA
10:00   Introductions and coffee
        Presentation of market research study
        Discussion of results
        Proposal for next stages
        Date of next meeting
11:30   Close
```

Formal meetings start with minutes of the previous meeting, main points arising from the meeting, additional reports or subjects and finish with 'AOB' (any other business).

7. Confirm the details in writing to participants – meeting place, date and time – by letter, fax or email, with the agenda.
8. The day before the meeting telephone all participants to ensure they will be attending and that they have all the information they need.
9. On the day of the meeting check the room is tidy with the right number of chairs and tables, technical equipment, availability of pens, paper and refreshments.
10. Ensure someone is responsible for taking notes, so that minutes can be written later. Minutes cover the basics of the meeting, and highlight 'action points' where people have agreed to do something.

How do I run a meeting?

An acceptable alternative to the term 'chairman' or 'chairwoman' is 'chair'. If you are given the task of chairing a meeting, do some homework beforehand. Make sure you know exactly who is coming, and whether they have particular views or objectives about points on the agenda.

Before the meeting starts introduce participants to each other if they haven't taken responsibility for this (see page 35 for introduction techniques), and make sure they have refreshments.

Start the meeting by reviewing who is present, the time available and the objective of the meeting.

That's the easy bit. Now people start talking – and the conversations can go in a multitude of directions. The really rude meeting participant might:

✘ talk too much, without knowing any facts
✘ interrupt people – implying that what they say is more important
✘ look bored or fall asleep

Business Etiquette *your questions and answers*

- ✖ make personal remarks
- ✖ run side conversations or tell private jokes
- ✖ lose their temper or show frustration
- ✖ be patronising to other people in the room.

The correct way of behaving at a meeting is to listen to all speakers, only interrupt through the chair at an appropriate moment, stick to the subject so not to waste the group's time, and only make sensible suggestions. Speak clearly – if you are interrupted ask to finish, but do not let it become a battle.

As the chair you won't have control about how people behave, but must attempt to keep the meeting on track, and ensure all participants have their say, without time being wasted. You should also take contentious subjects irrelevant to the meeting offline.

If you are discussing the budget for new furniture for the office reception, and the conversation has drifted to a review of the floral arrangements, gently bring the meeting back by saying, 'Shall we concentrate on the issue of new furniture first?'

If one person appears to be dominating the conversation you could say – 'David, in the interests of time I think we should move on through the agenda. Does anyone have further points to make on the magazine racks?'

To conclude the meeting the chair should summarise the comments and conclusions reached, confirm what the next actions will be and thank everyone for attending. If appropriate, you should ensure that the minutes will be typed and distributed to all those who who were invited to attend. The minutes will give them important information about decisions made and action points, even for those who couldn't be present.

How do I make introductions?

There are many different situations where people meet for the first time. Handling introductions well helps all the business conversations that follow. In a number of seconds you need to convey names and roles and relative status, so there is a lot of subtlety in how introductions are handled.

Start by thinking about how you introduce yourself. If you act in a confident, respectful and open way the first time you meet someone you will immediately create a good impression.

> 'Hello, my name is Celia Fate, from Automated Systems, and I'm here for a meeting with Mr Phil T Lucre in the payroll department.'
>
> 'Hello Mr Lucre, I'm Celia Fate from Automated Systems, I'm very pleased to meet you.'

Mr Lucre's status is recognised – he can choose to say 'please call me Phil' while Celia has indicated that she can be addressed by her first name.

Introducing individuals to each other is more complicated, but it is an important skill to learn, particularly for business meetings. Your aim is to put everyone at their ease by providing the names and roles and status of everyone present, and providing enough information so a conversation can be started.

It is polite to introduce a junior colleague to a more senior member of staff, introduce men to women, and introduce clients to colleagues. You will have to employ sensitive social antennae to know when to use titles or first names.

> 'Mr Senior, can I introduce you to Nahida Jobe who has just joined our customer support department as an administrative assistant. Nahida, Mr Senior is the Technology Director here at Cordless Communications.'
>
> 'Barbie, can I introduce Ken Ewin, our new account manager from the sales promotion agency Skretch & Kard. Ken this is Barbara Doll, the Marketing Manager of Cordless Communications.'

> 'Mr Cashriche, can I introduce Mr Senior our Technology Director at Cordless Communications. I'm sure he will be able to handle any of your outstanding concerns. Mr Senior, Mr Cashriche is the purchasing manager for the Sultan of Assi Dundil.'

If you are likely to be introducing VIPs or people with honorary or aristocratic titles then check the correct form of address with their private secretaries, or in a detailed book on etiquette.

What about going to conferences and exhibitions?

Sometimes it's necessary to go away from home and the office for work – to attend a conference or represent your company at an exhibition or trade fair. These are important functions in every industry, giving people a chance to keep up to date with developments, and meet others in the same field. But remember, they are essentially about work – a huge misjudgement is to think you've been given a free holiday and can make whoopee on expenses.

When you travel for business you are on show continually, so the right conduct is crucial. Indulging in sexual liaisons, copious alcohol, rushing naked down the hotel corridor at 3am in the morning and limited sleep should be reserved for the fortnight in Torremolinos. Otherwise you won't be able to do what you are paid for – which is represent your company.

Working on an exhibition stand is very gruelling. You need to stand all day in smart clothes and deal pleasantly with hundreds of strangers who are looking for free pens and other give-aways. Exhibitions and trade fairs are a good source of business for many companies so a professionally run stand is important.

It's likely that a manager will brief you on the dos and don'ts – here is a quick list.

✔ Keep the space tidy and free from litter.

Business Etiquette *your questions and answers*

- ✘ Don't eat, smoke or drink when you are on duty.
- ✔ Greet visitors in a friendly way and offer to help them.
- ✘ Never leave someone loitering aimlessly while you chat to your workmates.
- ✔ If you are tired organise breaks with your colleagues so the area is always manned.
- ✘ Don't take your shoes off, slouch in a chair, or stretch out in the meeting area for a quick kip.

Exhibitions and conferences usually have a lot of hospitality events organised, and they can be very tempting. But don't overdo the alcohol or food, especially if you are on duty, as you'll be very uncomfortable and not much use as a company representative.

How should I behave at a business lunch or dinner?

Often business people meet together over a meal. There are many reasons why such an event will be arranged – but they are primarily about developing personal relationships in a less formal setting than a meeting, by providing hospitality.

Breakfast meetings are increasingly popular ways for busy people to keep up their network of contacts and exchange ideas. They don't interfere with the working day and can be very casual.

Lunches are more formal and are used for getting to know individuals or companies you are working with. They are often arranged as a reward for work undertaken.

Business dinners have more ceremony, and generally mark important long-term relationships. Invitations often include partners.

The protocol for arranging lunches or dinners will vary depending on the group, and location. As a host you should:

1. Choose a venue that is convenient and has the right level of 'pomp'

depending on the event and the guest list. An overly expensive venue can be as awkward for guests as a greasy café.

2. Make sure seating is arranged so there is a balance of men and women, and different organisations are mixed. If all your colleagues are on one side of the table facing the suppliers you have invited it can feel like a war game.

3. Check that the menu caters for any special dietary requirements of the guests.

4. If wine is served, ensure it is chosen to complement the meal after the food has been ordered. White wine with fish and poultry, red wine with red meats. If you are not confident, find out if there is a wine expert in the party, or ask the restaurant's wine waiter for recommendations.

4. Make sure water and other soft drinks are available.

6. If the food is hot, ask guests to start eating as soon as the food is served.

Table manners

Good table manners go unnoticed; the mildest reaction to bad table manners is distaste, and it's often closer to downright revulsion. If you suspect your table manners aren't as good as they could be, get some advice on the correct use of cutlery and glassware etc, and follow these basic rules of polite table behaviour:

- ❏ Don't talk and eat at the same time, or chew with your mouth open.
- ❏ Don't stare at others while they eat. Whether through bad manners or cultural differences, some people will have habits at the table that are odd to you (for example North Americans might cut up all their food before starting to eat, some cultures think it's polite to burp afterwards). Remember that obvious curiosity or disgust from fellow diners makes people uncomfortable.
- ❏ Put your napkin in your lap, don't tuck it into your collar.
- ❏ Don't order anything that you know you will find difficult to eat tidily – for instance spaghetti, mussels, crab, artichoke globes, unfilleted

fish and snails all require a certain technique, and if you haven't got it, you'll end up with more food on your (or your neighbour's) clothing than in your stomach.

- If you can't resist the messy food, make occasional use of your napkin to discreetly wipe your mouth – or go to the toilets if more serious measures are needed. Don't get out a mirror at the table or indulge in any other personal grooming, like combing your hair or picking your teeth.
- Cutlery has different functions, depending on the course and type of food you are eating. If in doubt, work from the outside in and resist using your fingers.
- Sit up straight without slouching, and when eating move the food to your mouth with the implements provided. Don't move your mouth to your food by bending over your plate, or pick up plates or bowls to bring them closer to your face. (Unless, for instance, it's an oriental restaurant and you know the procedure.)
- Never lean across anyone to reach for condiments or drinks. Ask for them to be passed to you.
- Don't smoke during a meal, or while there is food on the table. When the food is finished and no one objects it is allowable – but always ask first.

What about business gifts?

Meals and hospitality are a form of generosity that is widely practised – apart from anything else they are good for networking and building relationships between suppliers and customers. Gifts are a grey area when it comes to business ethics. A brown envelope containing used banknotes from a potential supplier should *not* be accepted. There are many examples which are not so clear – the Christmas hamper or bottle of wine, the 'sample' computer, or tickets for a weekend in Paris.

Many organisations have guidelines setting the value of gifts that can be accepted and request that all gifts are listed. MPs, for instance, must publish their 'register of interests'. Government employees cannot accept gifts at all.

Use your common sense when being offered gifts by contacts. Is it a thank you, or is it a bribe? If in doubt, take the matter to a senior member of staff who should be able to advise you.

What business etiquette rules do I need to consider with international contacts?

If you are meeting with business people from other cultures – make sure you do your homework and know exactly how their business etiquette differs from accepted practices in the UK. Talk to colleagues or consultants with experience and contact the relevant government departments, which are set up to help international trade.

It is a good idea to employ a professional translator, if you are meeting with a wide range of people, but you should also learn about:

- Forms of address
- How greetings are made
- Customs for gifts and hospitality
- Body language and physical contact
- Cultural differences in use of language.

It's also important to be aware of the time frames others work in. You might be a 'morning' person, but someone who's just got off a 20-hour flight isn't going to be on your wavelength at 8am. Equally, expecting South Europeans to contribute much to a 2pm brainstorming session is not sensible – they usually have a long lunch break, so their bodies and minds will be accustomed to resting at this time.

Use your common sense, but find out what you can about your foreign visitor's likely habits. Two cultures that are very different from Britain are Japan and the Arab world. Here are some examples of common behaviour you must be aware of for successful business relationships.

Doing business with Japan

Everyone has seen films with the stereotype business executive so you know that introductions include elaborate rules about bowing, and adding the courtesy 'san' to the end of a name.

The Japanese have much more conservative codes of conduct and dress than Europe, so understanding the differences is important to avoid offence. Meetings and negotiations take time, and it's important to arrange groups of equal status. Management teams run companies, so decision-making is rarely instantaneous.

They react badly to criticism, any sign of distrust, or overt flattery. The Japanese culture very rarely uses the word 'no', so you need to be sensitive to responses that seem evasive or non-committal.

The Arab world

In the Middle East different rules apply. Arabs are much more tactile and seemingly relaxed. Exchange of greetings and pleasantries with hospitality precede any business discussion. Punctuality is not considered too important. This doesn't mean that they don't expect correct forms of address to be used, and appropriate business dress.

Usually alcohol is not served. The right hand only is used for eating, drinking and smoking. Business is not usually done on Holy Days and important Muslim festivals, but this can vary between Arab states.

6. Where can I find out more?

Is there any special training?

Social skills are largely gained by observation. You need to be aware of the people around you and be prepared to adapt to their way of behaving. So the main skill to learn is about assessing where you are, and whom you are with, and being polite. Learn from your colleagues and managers. Watch how the successful and well-regarded ones behave, and ask for advice – they will probably be flattered and only too pleased to help!

Débutantes go to finishing school to learn about the finer details of protocol and polite behaviour at banquets, receptions and weddings. For the majority of us it is about asking advice, and thinking what our parents or grandparents would say!

Who could I contact?

No organisations deal specifically with business etiquette. The following contacts can be useful sources of information on best practice, codes of conduct and employment issues.

The Department of Trade and Industry (DTI)
1 Victoria Street, London SW1H 0ET
Tel: 0171 215 5000
http://www.DTI.gov.uk
Business in Europe: 0117 944 4888

Health and Safety Executive
Rose Court, 2 Southwark Bridge, London SE1 9HS
Tel: 0171 717 6000

Institute of Management
2 Savoy Court, London WC2R 0EZ
Tel: 0171 497 0580
http://www.inst-mgt.org.uk

Investors in People UK
7–10 Chandos Street, London W1M 9DE
Tel: 0171 467 1900; Fax: 0171 636 2386

What publications should I look at?

There are many publications on correct behaviour, dealing with contacts, office policy and so on. Think about the particular skills you need to develop, and have a look in your local library for books such as these:

Debrett's new guide to etiquette and modern manners: The indispensable handbook, John Morgan, Headline 1996

Doing business in Japan, Jonathan Rice, Penguin 1995

Dos and taboos around the world, Roger Axtell, John Wiley 1993

Japanese business etiquette: A practical guide to success with the Japanese, Diana Rowland, Warner 1994

Mind your manners: Managing business cultures in Europe, John Mole, Nicholas Brearley 1995

Saying it right: How to talk in any social or business situation, William Glass, Perigree 1992

The complete book of business etiquette, Lynne Brennan and David Block, Piatkus 1991

The office jungle: The survivor's guide to the nylon shagpile of corporate life, Judi James, Harper Collins 1997

The simple guide to customs and etiquette in Arabia and the Gulf states, Bruce Ingham, Global 1994

After finishing university, you should be smart enough to spot a good deal when you see one.

As a graduate, we can offer you a first class package including:
- Special offers on graduate overdrafts and loans.
- Primeline, our 24 hour person-to-person telephone banking service.
- Commission-free travellers cheques and currency.
- And many other benefits.

If you'd like more details, simply call us on the number below.

0800 200 400
Monday-Friday 8am-8pm, Saturday 9am-6pm
www.natwest.co.uk

NatWest
More than just a bank

Credit is only available to persons over the age of majority and is subject to terms and conditions. Written quotations are available on request from National Westminster Bank Plc 41 Lothbury, London EC2P 2BP. Registered number 929027 England. We may monitor and record your phone calls with us in order to maintain and improve our service. Ref. No. TG98